MW00679257

HAUL A**
AND TURN LEFT

HAUL A**
AND TURN LEFT

THE WIT AND WISDOM OF NASCAR

MONTE DUTTON

WARNER BOOKS
New York Boston

If you purchase this book without a cover you should be aware that this book may have been stolen property and reported as "unsold and destroyed" to the publisher. In such case neither the author nor the publisher has received any payment for this "stripped book."

Copyright © 2006 by Monte Dutton
All rights reserved.

Warner Books
Time Warner Book Group
1271 Avenue of the Americas, New York, NY 10020
Visit our Web site at www.twbg.com.

Printed in the United States of America

First Warner Books Edition: February 2006
10 9 8 7 6 5 4 3 2 1

ISBN: 0-446-69668-4
ISBN-13: 978-0-446-69668-5
LLCN: 2005930622

Book design and text composition by Lili Schwartz
Interior illustrations by Matthew Marvin
Cover design by Flag
Cover illustration by Jeff Wong

To my colleagues in the racing press,
most of whom work exceedingly hard,
most of whom are honest and honorable,
and all of whom get less credit
than they deserve.

ACKNOWLEDGMENTS

Jim Cypher, my agent, has lent more guidance and assistance
than could be reasonably expected from the call of duty.

Several colleagues—David Poole, Mike Hembree, Kenny Bruce,
Jim McLaurin, Rick Minter, and Thomas Pope spring immediately to mind—
have made suggestions that ended up improving the text and
firing my memory and creativity.

Public relations representatives Dan Zacharias of Ford
and Ray Cooper of Dodge have been particularly helpful.

Jason Pinter of Warner Books established standards
of communication and cooperation that other publishers of my work
will have trouble matching.

No matter how much their sport grows, NASCAR fans feel a bit put upon by those who do not share the passion. Mike Watt, a fan from Edmonton, Alberta, says, "If you come to one of these races and don't have any idea what the big deal is, there's no way I'm ever going to be able to explain it to you."

NASCAR fans dismiss most of the rest of the mainstream sports as "stick-and-ball sports." It's a mild term of derision, this idea that Barry Bonds, Shaq, Peyton Manning and all the rest are occupying themselves with little boys' sports. Racers, on the other hand, are, to their fans, the righteous icons of the Great American Love Affair with the Automobile. Surrounded by steel, fuel, and rubber, they are the last true folk heroes in the eyes of their fans, who refer to them by their first names—Dale, Tony, Jeff, Mark, Rusty, and Mikey—and place them either on a pedestal or in a Dumpster, depending on where the allegiances fall.

Rick Larouse travels to the Nextel Cup race in Las Vegas every year from his home in the Canadian province of Alberta. What keeps him coming back? "The atmosphere," he says firmly, "and the character of the drivers. I like a man who calls it the way he sees it. I see that more in some of the veteran drivers, the ones who have been around. Some of the young drivers seem kind of plastic to me, but I'd be the first to admit that part of that's probably the fact that I don't know 'em as well.

"Don't matter who you are, though. It takes guts to drive a race car. Every one of 'em's a cut above the average Joe, if you ask me."

It's not a cult anymore, not even in western Canada. The average attendance at a Nextel Cup race is over 150,000. The TV ratings are second only to the National—buh-buh-buh-BUH!—Football League. The snobs can look down their noses if they want, it being a free country, but the gearheads with the "3" stickers in the back windows of their pickup trucks have earned the last laugh. The NASCAR army now regularly descends on virtually every outpost, great and small, and completely overruns it. For two weekends a year, even trendy Los Angeles cowers in the wake of the legions of fans who arrive from the heartland, wielding their beer coolers and charcoal grills as if they were weapons.

"What I love about NASCAR is the diversity," says Mo Curry, a fan from Philipsburg, Montana. "The diversity of the people is amazing. Let me explain what I mean by that. My husband and I towed our little camper down here [Las Vegas] from home. When we got here, we backed it in right next to a big motor coach that cost $200,000 if it cost a dime."

"America is built on wheels," adds her husband, Bo. "You know why more and more people are getting into NASCAR? You can relate. Everybody drives a car, and everybody wishes he could get in a race car and go fast."

Even as they rejoice, though, they feel a bit resented and underappreciated. Invariably, the major metropolitan dailies arrive on the scene with one of either two stories in mind. Either it's "the cultural phenomenon of the NASCAR dads," a term that happened along at least a decade after it became relevant, or "let's hang out in the infield with all the Bubbas." The latter is an easy story to write, stock car fans being good-humored sorts who will even laugh along when they are being ridiculed. Don't think they don't know what's happening, though. They know it's open season on Bubbas in Chicago, Frisco, and L.A. They know other groups in this country are practically immune to such satirical fire. They can take a joke, though, and that's a good thing.

"Who cares what people think? This is the biggest carnival on earth," says Bo Curry. "Unless you attend one of these things, you've got no idea what you're missing. The race is cool, but look at this midway. Look at all the souvenir trailers. You can spend all day out here, just watching the people."

"Y'all have to write whatever you have to write. Your opinions are yours, and you write them down on a piece of paper and share it with thousands of people. I've been criticized enough where y'all can't hurt me. You can't write anything that's going to make my day any worse. And you can't, all of a sudden, tell me I'm smart and great and make me feel any better. I didn't believe you when you said I sucked, and I'm not going to believe you when you say I'm great! I'm just going to keep on being me."

–MICHAEL WALTRIP
addressing the media after a second-place finish
at Phoenix in April 2005

"Sometimes, when Bruton opens his mouth, it sounds like he's constipated."

–WILLIAM C. FRANCE

NASCAR tycoon, on rival tycoon O. Bruton Smith

"I definitely think me and Michael [Waltrip] could whip their guys in a tag-team match."

–DALE EARNHARDT JR.

in reference to rival team Richard Childress Racing, at Daytona in 2003

"If Congress didn't pass a vote I wanted passed, I'd end up saying the first thing that came to my mind, and you can't do that. When Saddam challenged Bush to a public debate a few weeks ago, Bush didn't even acknowledge the challenge, because it wouldn't accomplish anything. It was petty. It was absolutely the right thing to do by not accepting Saddam's challenge. And that's why I couldn't be president, because not only would I have accepted it, I would've given him my calling-card number."

–JIMMY SPENCER

surprising no one by announcing he would not
be a candidate for president in 2004

"If we're going to keep fuel-mileage racing, we might as well build solar cars and let the sun decide who wins."

–TONY STEWART

"I'm glad I don't have to face a Randy Johnson fastball or a Warren Sapp hit when I'm releasing a pass, but I bet Tim Duncan is glad he's not running two hundred miles per hour with forty-two other cars around him, too."

–KYLE PETTY

"Wonder if they have boiled peanuts in California?"

–KEN SCHRADER

responding to California Speedway getting the Labor Day
weekend date once reserved for Darlington

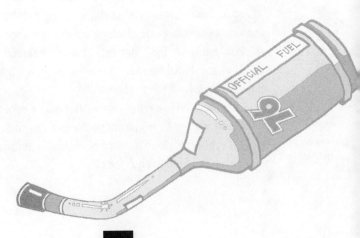

On a sunny afternoon in the garage area of Las Vegas Motor Speedway, ex-champions David Pearson and Tony Stewart got to know each other.

At the time, Pearson was seventy years old, Stewart thirty-three. Pearson's last championship occurred in 1969, when what is now Nextel Cup was referred to as Grand National and there were no races in Las Vegas.

Perhaps more than any of his contemporaries, though, Stewart is a throwback to the days when dinosaurs named Pearson, Richard Petty, Cale Yarborough, and Bobby Allison ruled the earth. Earth, at the time, mainly consisted of the South.

Pearson, who won 105 races, was leisurely strolling around with another notable resident of Spartanburg, South Carolina, former car owner and ace mechanic Walter "Bud" Moore. As luck would have it, they happened to be in front of the stall where Stewart's number 20 Chevrolet rested, shortly after the end of a practice session and as Stewart was climbing out of his orange car.

"Do you know Tony Stewart?" I asked Pearson.

"I've met him," he said. "I don't know him. I know he can sure enough drive a race car."

"I think you'd like him," I said. "Hang on a minute."

I then walked over in front of the car, where Stewart was discussing various matters of technical significance with his crew chief, Greg Zipadelli.

"David Pearson's out there," I said to Stewart. "Want to say hello?"

"Give me a minute," said Stewart.

I walked back out and started talking with Moore, about whose teams I used to write, and Pearson, the hero of my youth. The topic was familiar: how much times have changed, how not all the changes have been for the best, how much all the cars are just alike, etc. It was the kind of conversation old-timers have regardless of whether they're athletes or shoe salesmen.

Pearson looks as if he could climb right back into a stock car and run five hundred miles. He seems far more robust than a man who underwent open-heart surgery a few years back. He has the same barrel chest and broad shoulders he boasted when he was winning eleven races in eighteen tries in 1973.

After a few minutes of chitchat, though, the proud ex-champion was getting a little restless. With a small sense of urgency, I excused myself and returned to the garage stall, where Stewart had been intercepted by someone else.

"Hey, Tony," I said, "the best stock car racer who ever lived is out there, and I don't think I'd make him wait much longer."

Stewart looked up. "Don't let him get away," he said. "I'll be right there."

Thirty seconds may have passed before Stewart strode out into the desert sunshine.

"Hey," he said, shaking Pearson's hand, "I need you to drive my car for me at Darlington. I ain't worth a damn at that track."

Pearson didn't flinch. "All you got to do is drive that thing as high on the track as you can get it," he said.

"That's what I'm doing," Stewart said, smiling.

"You ought to have driven it when it was hard," replied Pearson, who won there a record ten times. "It's easy now."

By this time, a small army of photographers had descended, snapping what must have been hundreds of shots as another writer and I ducked out. I felt like saying, "Hey, guys, you're welcome."

After a reasonable period of photo ops taken while they chatted, Stewart and Pearson walked over to the Joe Gibbs Racing transporter and went inside to chat a while longer. Pearson came out with an autographed photo for his grandson, aptly named David.

Say what you want about Stewart, but he is nothing if not mindful of the past and respectful of its heroes. At any given time that he isn't embroiled in high-level discussions on just how he's going to manage to win the next race, a visit to Stewart's transporter will find him talking shop with a Red Farmer or a Donnie Allison. Stewart feels at home in the company of the hardscrabble men who preceded him.

No one needs to remind Pearson of how great he was. He's a proud man, but he's not one to elaborate on his great works and deeds. Pearson grew up in a textile mill village, and when he rose to prominence, he knew well the feeling of being looked down upon by the society folks. I wasn't kidding when I told Stewart he was the best stock car racer ever to strap on a helmet. That's my opinion and it's unlikely to change.

"They're going to have to change at least two right-side tires."

—NBC anchor

ALLEN BESTWICK

calling the 2002 Budweiser Shootout

"[Crew chief] Tommy Baldwin would like to say he's going to Disneyland, but actually, he'll be going to Rockingham next week with the rest of us."

—Motor Racing Network's

JOE MOORE

after Baldwin's driver, Ward Burton, won the 2002 Daytona 500

"Depends on the day."

–MATT KENSETH

asked what it was like to drive for Jack Roush

MONTE DUTTON

"It's been a whirlpool week."

—WARD BURTON

obviously meaning to say "whirlwind"

14

"I wonder a lot about what I would have been had my dad not been a race car driver. I'd probably have ended up in the cotton mill somewhere."

–DALE EARNHARDT JR.

"I can run ten miles. I don't think driving five hundred miles is going to be a problem."

–STEVE PARK

prior to making his comeback after suffering
a severe head injury in 2001

"I'll trade 'em [Chevrolet] three rule changes
for Jeff Gordon."

—Dodge owner
RAY EVERNHAM
once Gordon's crew chief

A nother driver who bridges the generation gap is Dale Earnhardt Jr., and, naturally, part of the reason is the legacy of his late father. Just being the Second Coming of Dale isn't enough, though. Earnhardt Jr. manages to be mindful of where he came from without coming across as a cheap imitation of his father. No one's ever going to call him Intimidator II. He's his own man, as distinct a representative of his own generation as a bearer of the family flame.

"I don't have near as much common sense as he had, and he banked on that just about all day, every day of his life," he says of his father.

Junior wears his caps backward, speaks with conviction of his hatred of bigotry, listens to music as loud and raucous as the growl of his Chevy V-8, and displays a disarming informality that is both popular with the ladies and appealing to the masses.

After all, it was Junior who, after winning the Daytona 500 in 2004, responded to a congratulatory call from George W. Bush by saying to the president of the United States, "It was real good to meet you today. Take it easy."

Wonder how many times Bush has had someone tell him to take it easy?

He finished second in the race in which his father lost his life, and, for a while, he mourned the loss of a man he had always loved but only recently come to understand. Like all men with the racing fever in their blood, he understood the need to climb back into the car and compete again.

In 2004, Earnhardt Jr. had to cope with personal adversity after being burned in a sports car crash. The brush with disaster may have slowed him a bit, but it was difficult to notice. Sounding very much like his old man, he scoffed at any notion that perhaps it might not have been prudent to take a chance by spending a weekend away from the stock car wars by racing on a road course.

"If the opportunity presented itself, and if they parked that [Corvette] C5 out there right now, I'd climb in it again," Earnhardt Jr. said. "It's what I do. I love to drive, and I love to race."

"Junior has gotten to that point where he reminds me a lot of his dad," said Jeff Gordon, a rival of both.

No one—not his father, not even Richard Petty—has ever been more popular with fans than Dale Earnhardt Jr. Each week his introduction is greeted wildly by grandstands as full of bright red, the color of Earnhardt Jr.'s car, as any Nebraska home crowd. His 2004 Daytona 500 victory occurred two years and 362 days after the death of his father. In other words, this pivotal NASCAR moment occurred three days shy of three years after the death of Number Three.

The son's rapid rise to prominence led some detractors to suggest that NASCAR officials were making it easy for Junior. He responded not with anger but rather a cool matter-of-factness.

"NASCAR couldn't run a legitimate business if there was a teacher's pet," he said.

He was just as apt later that same year when he pulled off a rather spectacular victory at the short track in Richmond, Virginia.

"For five minutes, I felt like my daddy," he said.

"[Owner] Richard Childress recently went polar-bear hunting up in the Northwest Territory near Antarctica."

—Fox commentator
LARRY McREYNOLDS

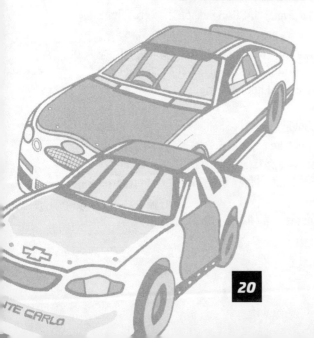

20

"We've got heavy hearts in the backs of our minds."

–KURT BUSCH

expressing his feelings on owner Jack Roush after Roush was injured in a 2002 plane crash

"I've always said your legacy is what you leave behind you."

–DARRELL WALTRIP

enlightening Fox TV viewers

"I drove down the middle, and I figured the hole was going to close. What I didn't figure, though, was that it was going to close on top of me."

—MICHAEL WALTRIP

describing a twenty-nine car pileup in a 2002
Busch Series race at Talladega

Harry Gant, who retired after the 1994 season, is mystified by autograph seekers, though even today he signs more than his share.

"Damnedest thing I've ever seen," says Gant. "These people will line up down the street in the pouring rain, just to get me to sign my name on a piece of paper or a postcard.

"You know, I always liked Elvis, but I didn't rightly care how he signed his name. I'd like to have known him. I wouldn't have minded singing along with him, or at least hearing him sing, but get his autograph? Nah."

Stock car racing has seldom seen a hero less affected by success than Gant, who still lives in his home-town, Taylorsville, North Carolina. Gant used to run a steakhouse there, and he is also a cattleman and an accomplished woodworker. When Gant retired, other drivers asked him if he was still going to be around at the track.

"Heavens, no," he replied. "You ever seen the traffic around these places? I built myself a piece of furniture for my television set. I can roll the set right out on my deck and watch the race right out there in the fresh air if I see fit."

"Seven hundred and fifty thousand dollars is a lot of money, but it … wouldn't have been worth what I had to do to get it."

–DALE EARNHARDT JR.

**explaining why he resisted the temptation to spin out
Ryan Newman in the 2002 all-star race, the Winston**

"I bumped him; that's part of it. I think we needed a yellow so we could put on a good show there at the end."

–KURT BUSCH

after not resisting the temptation to spin
Robby Gordon out in the same race

"Lowe's Motor Speedway is one of those tracks where the sun usually sets in the west."

—Motor Racing Network's

BARNEY HALL

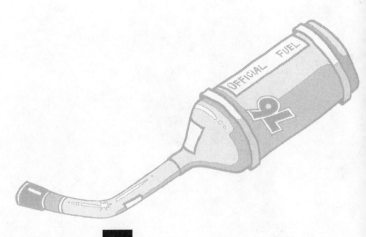

"Maybe if Jeff Gordon had been a little braver, he might've won."

–*KEVIN HARVICK*

after being told that Gordon, who finished second at
Chicagoland Speedway in 2002, had called his
driving through the grass "a stupid move"

Kurt Busch, the 2004 Nextel Cup champion, is fond of big words, of which there are some that he actually knows the meaning. Busch is kind of like the kid who went off to college for a year and came home thinking he knew everything. In fact, he did attend the University of Arizona for a year.

The owner of Busch's number 97 Ford, Jack Roush, also likes stringing syllables together, but Roush's use of the language is far more authoritative than that of his young driver. The truth is that Roush is probably a bad influence, linguistically, on Busch. Busch, if prompted, would probably say Roush was a bad influence "vocabularically."

After a qualifying run, Busch once said he had "circumferenced the track." After Ryan Newman's first pole of 2005, Busch called Newman's Dodge "ludicrous fast."

During Daytona Speedweeks in 2003, he said rival team DEI (Dale Earnhardt Incorporated) had "a threshold on the front of the competition." He added that "the DEI cars have some sort of wrath that nobody else has." He said of own his team, "It's real solidifying to know that the group is solid."

Hard to argue with that.

Referring to his spectacular sophomore season (in NASCAR, not college) which included three victories in the final five 2003 races, Busch said, "It's been somewhat of a tailspin and somewhat more of a comfort level to know what I'm capable of and to know where the team is at right now."

"Sorry teams don't usually win the Brickyard,
or anywhere else, if you think about it."

–MARK MARTIN

"I've got some really good words for him. Unfortunately, I can't say them on TV. I wish I had something I could've shot at him."

—*WARD BURTON*

angry at Dale Earnhardt Jr. after a crash
at Bristol in August 2002

"The Chevrolet has had more nose jobs than Michael Jackson."

–STERLING MARLIN
complaining about a NASCAR rules change

No one ever outran Ernie Irvan, who retired in 1999, in a race of verbal blunders. The best example occurred in a telephone press conference in 1997, shortly after Irvan had been told by Robert Yates that he would no longer drive Yates's number 28 Ford after that season.

With an army of journalists listening in, Irvan said, "You know what they say: When the going gets tough, the tough get happening."

When asked if Yates had given him a reason for his dismissal, Irvan said, "Well, you know, I went to Robert, and he didn't really give me a reason. He just hee-hawed around the subject."

Then a reporter asked Irvan if he was concerned at being "a lame duck."

"Somebody asked me that the other day, and I didn't really know what the guy meant," Irvan replied. "I never played baseball when I was a kid."

In the span of about ninety seconds, Irvan had dozens of reporters laughing uncontrollably, heads facedown in their computer keyboards, punching the table with their fists.

"We had the wrong gear, wrong springs, wrong shocks, and wrong car. We had the right beer, but other than that, we got stomped."

—STERLING MARLIN

sponsored by Coors Light, at Dover in September 2004

"When I was twenty-two or twenty-three, I was trying to act like I was forty-five or fifty. I'm not saying that didn't help me get a long way in this sport, but, now that I'm thirty-one, going on thirty-two, I want to get back some of those years."

—JEFF GORDON
before the 2003 Daytona 500

"Fast and smooth. You don't have to be aggressive as long as you're fast and smooth."

–RYAN NEWMAN

Jeff Gordon was not always the self-assured, polished spokesman he is today. When he was in his early twenties, he had become a superstar on the track but remained uncertain off it. He often relied on the protective influence of crew chief Ray Evernham and drove journalists mad with responses that seemed rehearsed and predictable.

In 1995, when Gordon was closing in on his first championship, he conducted a press conference at Atlanta Motor Speedway, which then hosted the final race of the season. Journalists were informed in advance that Gordon would not answer any question concerning the championship and would only respond to questions specifically referring to the specific race. This stipulation, of course, defeated the purpose of holding a press conference.

It took a resourceful writer to smoke Gordon out.

Jim McLaurin, then covering NASCAR for *The State* newspaper in Columbia, South Carolina, was up to the task.

"Jeff," he said, "I know you won't answer any questions about the championship. What I want to know is why you won't answer any questions about the championship."

Most everyone in the room erupted in laughter. Gordon couldn't keep a straight face. And he did talk about the championship he would wrap up two days later.

"He drives off the end of his hood. He can't see past his ears."

—TERRY LABONTE

referring to Kurt Busch after an Indianapolis crash in 2003

"If we ever had fan interference in this sport, it'd be a lot worse than a dropped ball."

–KEN SCHRADER

noting the controversial incident in the
2003 Cubs–Marlins baseball playoff series

"We all knew what the deal was when we got into it. It's not like we started a five-day-a-week, nine-to-five job and all of the sudden somebody said, 'Hey, we need you working more hours, traveling all over the country, and being gone just about every weekend.' This didn't surprise anyone. When we signed up we knew how many weeks, how many races, had a pretty good idea of where they were going to be, and knew what we had to do. Nobody fooled us into it."

–KYLE PETTY

Before the start of the 2005 season, I asked Carl Edwards if anyone had ever told him he was so wholesome and enthusiastic it made them sick.

This youthful believer in truth, justice, and the American way replied, "Oh, yeah. I get that all the time."

Twenty-five years, Edwards's age at the time, might be a relatively mature length of age for some, but not for race drivers, who strap themselves into outrageously fast vehicles and live out their frenetic dreams. Missouri gave the world Tom Sawyer and Huck Finn, and Edwards—from Columbia, Missouri, not Mark Twain's Hannibal—is descended from that fictional heritage.

It's not hard to imagine Edwards, sitting in some high school classroom, daydreaming about winning the Daytona 500. He's all "yes, sir" and "no, sir," reciting his sponsors even to an audience of world-weary journalists who wouldn't mention Scotts fertilizer (one of Edwards's sponsors) if they were standing up to their knees in a weed-infested garden.

Come to think of it, it wouldn't be hard to imagine Edwards daydreaming even now—that is, except for the fact that he's living out his dreams with the world as his witness.

Jeff Gordon has his own brand of wine. Carl Edwards deserves his own line of comic books. He couldn't get a movie deal because his story is too hokey. In a way, it's a shame that Edwards isn't an actor because, now that Mickey Rooney's day is past, he alone could play Andy Hardy. If Jack Roush could build Edwards a Ford out of Lincoln Logs, he'd try to race it. Edwards is one of the last people alive who could say, "Gee whiz, that's swell," and keep a straight face.

The occasion of Edwards's first Nextel Cup victory, the Golden Corral 500 at Atlanta Motor Speedway on March 20, 2005, was just as hokey, uplifting, and, well, swell as everything else about him.

"I was trying to get by Jimmie [Johnson], which is just about impossible," said Edwards after doing so on the final lap. "It just worked out at the end. I can't believe it worked out."

The thing is, when Edwards says something, despite the fact that it's sickeningly wholesome, it's impossible not to believe him because, well, he delivers the goods, whether it's executing a backflip off the roof of his car or an otherworldly pass of the most productive NASCAR driver of recent vintage.

Anyone other than Edwards would be laughed out of the room. Somehow, in an age when all the various and sundry icons—Mark McGwire, Martha Stewart, Rush Limbaugh, Bill Clinton, maybe even Jeff Gordon—are being brought to their knees, Edwards lifts us up with his wide-eyed charm and makes us believe in the aforementioned truth, justice, and the American way again.

And that backflip! Edwards almost slipped up at Atlanta, completed as it was just a day after the one he wowed a smaller crowd with after his first Busch Series victory.

"The first time I saw him do it, I thought it was luck," said Jack Roush, the owner of Edwards's number 99 Ford. "I went over and said, 'We're going to be doing this a long time, and if you keep doing that, and rely on luck to do it, it's not going to work.'

"[Edwards] said, 'Don't worry. When I was in college, I had a girlfriend who would help me with it, and I was in a padded room, and I fell a lot, but now I won't fall down. I can do it.' It's not bragging if you can do it, and he's been doing it really well."

That observation could be made both of Edwards's backflips and his driving, but, of course, he doesn't brag about either. He even credits Tyler Walker, then a sprint car driver but now in the Busch Series, with giving him the idea for the celebratory backflips.

Heck, Edwards even thanked the media: "I just want to thank you guys because you've written some really nice things about me . . . and I know it won't always be good. There'll be times when you have to write bad things about me, and I'll be grateful for that, too."

That alone ought to be enough to make NASCAR officials dock him twenty-five, or even fifty, points. Thank a sponsor, okay, but thank the media? Them's fightin' words.

"Not to discredit them in any way, but NASCAR has become this black hole sucking up sponsorship, fans, TV viewers, and all the things that make racing work. It's like a giant vacuum cleaner. So how everybody gets along with reduced crowds, reduced money, and reduced ratings to me is the real issue. Look at what many others perceive as the crisis in open-wheel racing; a lot of that has to do with NASCAR just taking over the audience."

—DAVE DESPAIN

host of Speed Channel's *Wind Tunnel*

"I couldn't tell what was coming out of that little 'yap-yap' mouth of his."

–RICKY RUDD

referring to Kevin Harvick, after a post-race
altercation at Richmond in 2003

"I was about to get fired and Bill was getting old."

–JEREMY MAYFIELD

asked why his and teammate Bill Elliott's performances improved late in the 2003 season

I've never understood why there seems to be some innate compulsion to ask journalists to predict things: races, games, champions, political outcomes, etc. No one should expect us to play Nostradamus. What I'm trained to do is write about what's already happened. I don't have dreams of the future. I don't keep tea leaves handy. Normally, supernatural visions do not hover above my bed when I awaken in the middle of the night. Nature is usually what beckons when I awaken at such times. When someone—sadly, it's often another journalist—asks me to predict the winner of the Nextel Cup championship, I do it but I don't attach any particular importance to it.

I have, however, thought about it, and what I've concluded is that picking the champion under the current system is patently ridiculous. It's like deciding which numbers to select on a lottery ticket. Once the race-offs begin, it's kind of a crapshoot. It seems to me, though, that a more valid assessment would be to pick which ten drivers will have a chance to win that pulse-quickening, spine-tingling, maddeningly unfair "Chase."

Getting in the top ten after twenty-six races is what counts. Then it's a matter of getting hot, keeping the fenders uncrumpled, and hoping a rod doesn't fly through the cylinder wall. In 2004, Jimmie Johnson won four of the final ten races, but that wasn't enough to win the championship because Kurt Busch finished in the top ten in nine of them. Busch's persistence and tenacity were admirable, but it didn't hurt that, when the right front tire flew off his Taurus in the season's final race, it conveniently did so at the mouth of pit road and the tire itself continued rolling down the frontstraight, thus bringing out a caution flag, while Busch was guiding the car three-wheeled into his pit stall.

Making all the right moves isn't enough. It takes a little stardust.

"It's like you're sitting in a parking lot, a lot of times in the middle of a parking lot . . . This parking lot just happens to be going really, really fast."

–KEN SCHRADER

on racing at Talladega Superspeedway

"It was too crazy for me, and I'm 'bout the craziest one out there."

—DALE EARNHARDT JR.

after a Talladega race in 2003

"If the Romans had any sense, they would've
built Bristol instead of the Colosseum."

–O. BRUTON SMITH

chairman, Speedway Motorsports Inc.

American sport has no more ambitious a leader than NASCAR chairman Brian Z. France, but the youthful leader of this still-burgeoning sport is not without his eccentricities. When he is speaking in front of an audience, France's hand gestures can be metaphorically linked to a fifteen-car Talladega pileup.

France, the grandson of NASCAR's founder, makes frequent use of the old Bill Clinton thumbs-up gesture, but he has cultivated his own variations. Comparing the ex-president's mannerisms to France's is like comparing a triple-pump reverse dipsy-doo to a standard slam dunk. France is fond of firing the left thumb off to the side, making it appear as if he is referring to someone or something that invariably isn't there. Sometimes he fires one hand jauntily while karate-chopping with the other. The words are fraught with euphemisms, but the hands are charismatic.

When France steps up to a microphone, he sounds almost like he's starring in an infomercial. NASCAR exists, he says, "to showcase the opportunities for the best drivers in the world to do their thing." Those very same drivers invariably "step up to the plate" and "the more there is on the line," the better they perform.

Occasionally he misspeaks. In 2004, he noted that "it reeks [did he mean 'wreaks'?] of the whole industry to be able to absorb that many changes." Perhaps this was because "with momentum comes anticipation."

Shortly after he said this, a bus that had been pro-
vided for the convenience of journalists covering France's
momentous remarks returned from NASCAR's Research
and Development Center to a nearby hotel. As the bus
neared the hotel, one of the writers pointed to the roof of
another hotel, where a windblown stick figure was gyrat-
ing just about as wildly as Brian France. Apparently it was
atop the hotel because of a business conference being
held there.

"The answer, my friend, is Brian in the wind," the
writer said.

"When you're looking at me, you're looking at NASCAR history."

—RICHARD PETTY

who won two hundred Cup races,
nearly twice as many as anyone else

"You know how you get in shape to drive a race car? You drive a race car."

—DICK TRICKLE

Road racer Boris Said learned some lessons in his first Daytona 500.

"I love this kind of racing," he said, "[but] these guys sure change their personalities in race mode. They're like Doberman pinschers with a hand grenade in their mouths."

Joe Gibbs is a member of the Pro Football Hall of Fame who may well wind up in the NASCAR equivalent one day as well. He's won NFL championships as a coach and NASCAR titles as an owner.

"The Coach" considers the most notable difference between pro football and stock car racing to be the immediacy of the fans:

"This sport is so unusual in that aspect," he says of NASCAR. "I think that's what I love the most about it. In football, the players have very little contact with the fans. You take a bus to the stadium, you warm up, you play the game, you get back on the bus, and then you're gone. Where else can you have contact with your favorite athlete on the day of the event? It's not unusual for these guys [in NASCAR] to sign autographs and interact with the fans on the day of the race."

"You've got to be at least five feet tall and have a briefcase full of cash under both arms."

–DAVID PEARSON

who won 105 NASCAR races, asked what it takes to be a race car driver today

"It was wild out there, like cannibals chasing a deer."

–JERRY NADEAU

after a race at Atlanta Motor Speedway

"Short-track racing is like walking through a minefield. You have to watch every move and be completely aware of what's going on around you. If you give the guy in front of you some room, you'll get booted from behind. You can get bit by a lot of things you didn't have anything to do with starting."

–DALE EARNHARDT JR.

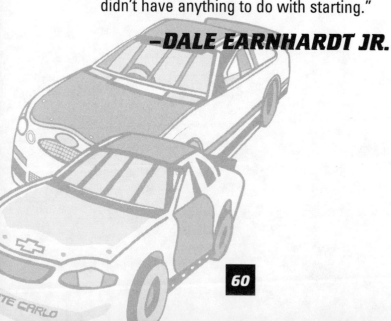

There are no more anxiously awaited Nextel Cup races than the two held annually at Bristol Motor Speedway. While a ticket to the August night race is a bit tougher to procure than the Sunday afternoon race in the spring, both are sold out well in advance. Fan polls invariably rate Bristol as the circuit's most popular track.

Yet the imposing short track in the Tennessee mountains doesn't seem to get the credit it deserves. It's amusing when national magazines touch on the subject of "tough tickets" and intimidating venues without mentioning Bristol.

Think the ACC basketball tournament is tough to see in person? If you want to attend that event—or at least most of it—just hang out at the exits when the fans of first-round losers are returning to their vehicles. Getting a ticket at face value for the rest of that affair is no problem. Bristol, on the other hand, will draw more than 100,000 for a Busch Series undercard. Many fans will roll into town with no assurance of seeing the Cup race, and they won't be too disappointed if they have to settle for one live and the other via television. A Yankees–Red Sox ticket is tough to finagle, but neither Yankee Stadium nor Fenway Park has 156,000 seats.

The retired car owner Bud Moore once described Bristol disparagingly as "a damn pinball machine," adding,

"It ought to be against the law to have more than two dozen cars running around that place at the same time."

But forty-three cars take the green flag, many of which won't last too long at the track where Sterling Marlin described the racing as "jet planes in a gymnasium."

There are too many cars going too fast in too small a space. That, in a nutshell, is what makes the fans love it.

"It's one of my favorites," says Tony Stewart, "but Bristol is a track that's feast or famine. If you have a really good day, it's a lot of fun, but if you have one little problem, it normally makes for a very long day."

Stewart speaks from experience. He's won there, but a graph of his finishes could've been charted at a seismic lab.

"You just don't have time to relax," he adds. "Everything happens so fast. At the end of the day, when the race is done and your adrenaline wears off, you're worn out, but when you're in the car and the adrenaline's pumping, you don't get in that smooth, calm rhythm like you do at a place like Michigan or California, where you've got big, sweeping corners and long straightaways.

"You don't get that luxury at Bristol. It's standard short-track racing."

Standard short-track racing? It's more like standard bedlam. Winners have crossed the finish line sideways or backward. Imagine roller derby with four skates. Imagine bobsledding with engines.

You want crashes? They occur inevitably on the tight concrete ribbon. On the one hand, the level of excitement would seem to suggest that the likely winner is the one lucky enough not to have three or four cars spin out in front of him. On the other, the results seem to indicate that some drivers have an otherworldly knack for staying clear of trouble.

It evidently takes some mystical brand of skill to succeed amidst the dizzying action at a track that is breathtakingly fast, incredibly small, and surrounded by grandstands banked even more steeply than its turns.

"When I saw the wall coming through the car, I knew I was in trouble."

—Busch Series driver

MIKE HARMON

after walking away from a gruesome crash at
Bristol Motor Speedway in 2002

"When I was coming along, if we went to the veteran drivers, it was for advice and because we looked up to them. I'm not sure that's the case in this day and time. A lot of young drivers come in with a little bit of a chip on their shoulder, thinking that's the way that they have to be . . . There's a little lack of respect, but it's not just in this garage area or not just within auto racing. It's in our society, period."

—DALE JARRETT

"I look at it the same way any weekend. If you play it too aggressive, it's going to get you in trouble. If you play it too conservative, it's going to get you in trouble. It doesn't matter where you're at."

–JEFF GORDON

"It's pretty nice, actually. I got a little confused a few weeks ago. I needed to go to the mall about the time the race started, and got there and thought, what are all these people doing here? I thought everybody watched the race. I'm learning there's a whole new world out there."

–TERRY LABONTE

after deciding to compete in just ten races a year

"I've lived it. I've done it. I like running more on my schedule than having to be there full-time."

–BILL ELLIOTT
explaining why he decided to cut back

"When I'm an old man, I'm going to bore my grandkids to death with racing stories, and I'll tell them once a week how I shocked everybody my rookie year by winning the Texas race. They'll probably be like, 'You told us that yesterday.'"

–DALE EARNHARDT JR.

During the week after his first Nextel Cup victory, Carl Edwards rang the opening bell at the New York Stock Exchange. The prospect sent him into what can only be described as a wide-eyed tizzy.

Edwards recalled, "I was like, 'I'm going to be in Columbia [Missouri, his hometown], and I don't know how I'll get there,' and she [public relations rep Sheri Hermann] said, 'No, you don't understand. Scotts is going to fly a private jet to pick you up in Columbia and fly you up there.' I was like, okay, that sounds great.

"So I told my little brother, Kenny, and he wanted to go. He has one suit and one nice shirt, so he threw that on, and we jumped on the plane and laughed all the way to New York. We were giddy the whole time, just thinking how different things are now from a couple of years ago. We had a limo and got to ring the bell. We got to hang out with members of the stock exchange, and they were all great people. It was unbelievable."

"There's no doubt in my mind the right decision was made to award Texas with a second Cup race. The facility is first-class, the fans are great, and they pack the place year after year. I'm a native of North Carolina, and I'll be the first to say I hate to see races being moved from my home state and other places in the Southeast. But the fact is that we already have a lot of races in the Southeast and some of them don't fill the grandstands now. Fans can best voice their opinion by purchasing tickets, and that's what the fans have done in Texas."

–*BRIAN VICKERS*

"It's the same for every track: a good-handling race car."

–DALE JARRETT

on what it takes to win

"The mayor told me one thing about him being on the city council. There haven't been nearly as many arguments."

–BOBBY LABONTE
whose stern father, Bob, is a Trinity,
North Carolina, alderman

"The cars are obviously much harder to drive, and it plays right into our drivers' hands . . . When you get around other cars, you don't have as much margin as they had before, and it depends on how hungry you are. If you're hungry enough, you go get it."

—team owner
JACK ROUSH
after his drivers won four of the first eight races during the 2005 season

Fans of both NASCAR and other sports often wonder aloud why the most prestigious event, the Daytona 500, opens each season. The only reason it's an issue is that other sports hold championships, naturally, at the end of seasons. Stock car racing can't really be compared to sports like football, baseball, and basketball, though. The means by which championships are decided is completely different in those sports. No one ever complains about the Masters or Wimbledon being contested near the beginning of the year.

The beginning of the NASCAR season finds every team at its peak. New cars have been freshly built and tested. Teams are fresh and rested. The relatively brief off-season gives everyone, including the fans, a chance to recharge and anticipate a new year.

Dale Jarrett said he wondered why anyone would do it any other way. The 2005 Super Bowl was played in Jacksonville, Florida, only a nine-minute drive from Daytona Beach, and it occurred at just about the time all the race teams were converging on the area. Jarrett was one of several NASCAR luminaries who attended the Super Bowl.

"There are a lot of comparisons," said the three-time Daytona 500 winner and 1999 Cup champion. "I think ours makes a lot of sense in having our biggest event be the first one of the year because everybody is the best prepared. We've had the most time to work and get ready for the Daytona 500, and it's our biggest race.

"I found it kind of amusing to be at the Super Bowl. I don't know the exact figures of how many people were there, but I would guess it was somewhere close to 100,000 people that actually attended the Super Bowl. We've got nearly 200,000 people here at the Daytona 500, and we have thirty-five other races that have [big] crowds, too."

The average attendance at Nextel Cup events exceeds 160,000.

The honorary starter of the 2005 Daytona 500 was actor Ashton Kutcher. He went into painstaking detail describing the demands of waving the green flag.

"I'm going to wave that flag like it's never been waved before," he said. "I started about a month ago on a regimen, stretching my wrist. It's all in the wrist. I started icing my wrist for a couple hours a day and built a Plexiglas box that I keep it in while I'm sleeping so I don't roll over on it.

"About a week ago, I started thinking about it, and I started getting really peeved because they didn't have me wave the checkered flag, which I thought would be more entertaining and fun. Then I realized that when you wave the checkered flag, you only make one person happy. When you wave the green one, you make millions of people happy. It's a pretty big gig."

Matthew McConaughey, the grand marshal, didn't know what to expect when he entered the speedway grounds.

"I had no idea of the size or scope," he said. "I went to school at the University of Texas at Austin, and we put 90,000 in the seats on Saturdays, and I get here and find out really quickly that this'll double that."

"At my age, I enjoy being out of the sun, and the idea of not getting my nose burned and my bald head scalded when we're having a race going on is a good thing, and racing tonight will mean that I won't fly home tonight by myself, I'll spend the night, and that's probably safer for everybody that's in the air."

–JACK ROUSH
explaining why he likes night races

"I'm a big component of night races."

–GREG BIFFLE

apparently meaning to say "proponent"

"I know one thing: When you're a driver, and you're struggling in the car and trying to get your car handling right, you're looking for God to come out of the sky and give you a magical answer."

–RUSTY WALLACE

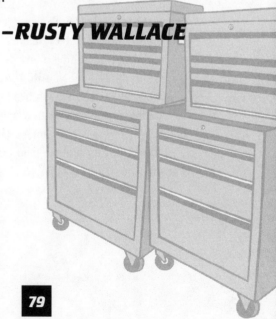

he wittiest sportswriter covering NASCAR is undoubtedly the Nashville *Tennessean*'s Larry Woody. A decorated Vietnam veteran, Woody is a master of the one-liner.

During a 2004 race at Atlanta Motor Speedway, Woody and another writer were commiserating the lack of action.

"This may be the most boring race I've ever seen," Woody observed.

"Well, look at the bright side," said the other writer. "I just completed my federal income tax."

Without blinking, Woody replied, "I just taught myself Portuguese."

Some tracks hold preliminary races sanctioned by the Automobile Racing Club of America, an Ohio-based sanctioning body whose drivers are typically adept at short tracks. Understandably, ARCA races on large, high-banked ovals are often crash-filled.

During one such event, Woody watched a multicar crash from his press-box vantage point.

"ARCA drivers are like mud turtles," Woody opined. "You can't hurt 'em."

"Where are we going next week? Talladega.
I'm going to see the '8' car in front of me all
day, so they'll be fine."

–KURT BUSCH
asked if Dale Earnhardt Jr. "had his act together"

"Whenever he doesn't run into somebody, I'm almost happy no matter what happens."

–JACK ROUSH

asked about the success of Carl Edwards

Richard Petty once helped organize the Professional Drivers Association, a short-lived organization whose members boycotted a 1969 race in Talladega, Alabama. Petty wasn't particularly sympathetic, though, thirty-six years later when some drivers called for NASCAR to implement a pension plan.

The seven-time champion said today's drivers earn $1 million by walking from "the bathroom to the car."

"I used to wonder what I was going to do when I gave up driving," said the King. "That was when it took me fifteen years to earn my first million dollars. From that standpoint, it looks to me like they need to look out for themselves."

"Yeah, I mean, regardless of this year or whatever, you get what you give. You party hard, you play hard, and that's what we do."

–DALE EARNHARDT JR.

"I don't see how a driver can allow his crew chief to make all the decisions when the crew chief doesn't ever drive the car."

–GREG BIFFLE

T

he late Dale Earnhardt Sr. had a clever way of getting NASCAR's attention. When Earnhardt was miffed at the ruling body's officials, he would stroll from his transporter over to NASCAR's mobile headquarters and begin signing autographs. Within minutes, the area would be awash in fans as word quickly spread that Earnhardt was signing autographs. The influx of humanity quickly disrupted any business being transacted at the command center.

After suffering several flat tires at a race on the old Riverside, California, road course in the early 1980s, Bobby Allison suggested that rival Darrell Waltrip's car owner, Junior Johnson, might have had a sharpshooter posted on high ground to shoot out the tires.

When informed of the charge, Johnson drawled, "If I'd had me a gun, I wouldn't have been shooting at his tires."

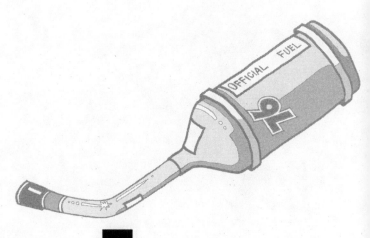

"The good thing about night races is that I get to sleep in in the morning."

–TONY STEWART

"Me getting by him would have been a stroke of genius."

–DALE EARNHARDT JR.

after finishing second to Tony Stewart in the
2002 Budweiser Shootout

"NASCAR has proven time and time again that they're willing to change the rules at any time for any or no reason . . . I don't get too excited about rules anymore because they could change at any time."

–TONY STEWART

Forget about the orthodox means of comparing sports venues. In NASCAR, those standards don't apply. A racetrack isn't a stadium. It doesn't provide residency to a home team. Comparing the track—or for that matter, the area that surrounds it—to a stadium, or a coliseum, or a park isn't just comparing apples to oranges. It's apples to pumpkins. Or horses. Or rivers.

It's not unusual for these races to draw fans from all over the country, not to mention the next country. A lady in the ticket office said Martinsville Speedway drew fans from "all fifty states."

Undoubtedly the Dallas Cowboys and the New York Yankees occasionally draw fans from, say, Jamaica, but there probably aren't any individual games that include fans from all fifty states. In fact, the Cowboys and Yankees seldom play games in front of fans from more than fifteen or twenty states.

People don't make road trips to NASCAR races. They make pilgrimages.

"I know Cup is bigger, but that's a joke."

—Busch Series driver

RANDY LAJOIE

noting that the winner of the series's Daytona race earned less than the last-place finisher in the Daytona 500

When Ricky Rudd first drove at Martinsville Speedway, in 1975, he was called on in relief of veteran driver Bill Champion, then in the twilight of his career. Rudd had raced on a couple of the longer tracks but had come just to watch the race when Champion sent word that he needed someone to finish for him.

Rudd, who got his start in go-karts, had never driven a stock car on a short track. Any short track.

"I never had so many fists shaken at me in one day in my life," he recalled. "That was a very memorable experience. It's what I remember about my first Martinsville race. That probably wouldn't be allowed to happen today, I guess."

"The playing field has never been level, and it sure ain't this time . . . NASCAR looks at it different than racers. NASCAR looks at it like a show: 'We need to throw the checkered flag at the end of five hundred miles, and forty-three cars need to be running side by side' . . . We want to try to get the edge . . . This year they've been jacking around with the rules like they do every year. It's going to be good for somebody, and it's going to hurt somebody. There's no way of making it even all the way through."

—seven-time Winston Cup champion
RICHARD PETTY

"Darlington is like Rockingham, only with no place to go."

–JOHN ANDRETTI

In racing, variety is truly the spice of life.

It's great that every track isn't just like Michigan, even though a bunch of them are. Oh, some of them are two miles and some are one and a half, but it greatly detracts from the appreciation of Michigan that it's so similar to California, which is similar to Las Vegas, Kansas City, and Chicagoland. Chicagoland, of course, is that wondrous term that includes Joliet, Illinois, which is only slightly less dissimilar to Chicago than Hooterville.

Then there's the "Bruton clone," Charlotte, which is much like Atlanta and Texas. Once upon a time, Atlanta was unique in that it was a "true oval" (not to be confused with a "true freshman") with wide, sweeping turns. The turns are still there, but now they're accompanied by Mr. Smith's truncated tri-oval, which he prefers to call a "quad oval," which makes about as much sense as calling Joliet "Chicagoland."

But they haven't quite stomped, battered, and pummeled all the variety out of NASCAR . . . yet.

Darlington is the most unique of all. Its racing groove, when compared to the wide, smooth comfort of the Michigan clones, is a sidewalk. It's the greatest test of driving ability. Not surprisingly, given the current mind-set that seems to govern the future of NASCAR, its future is endangered. Rockingham and North Wilkesboro have gone the way of the dinosaurs. Darlington is the spotted owl. Leaving Darlington with one date and making that date Mother's Day weekend is about like reestablishing the spotted owl's habitat as the L.A. freeways.

Phoenix is, like Darlington, odd. Fortunately, its oddness is located near a huge western city. Huge western cities have become the Wal-Marts of NASCAR. They're taking over the marketplace and running the "mom and pop" tracks, i.e., Darlington, Rockingham, North Wilkesboro, and other oddities to be named later, out of business.

But Phoenix is just fine, even if it is about as flat as a Dr Pepper left out in the sun with the cap off, and even though its back straight is as whop-sided as a two-dollar baseball after a line drive.

Bristol is high-banked, concrete-covered madness. Pocono has three straights, all of different distances, and three curves, all of different banking. Martinsville is the world's largest paper clip. Infineon (Sears Point) is a NASCAR version of the old country song that says "up this hill and down . . . and up this hill again."

"The track is so fast, it's not made for racing.
It's made for speed."

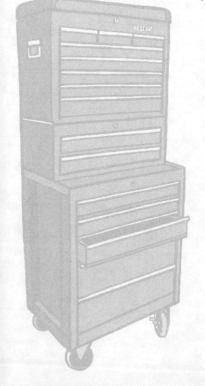

—RYAN NEWMAN

on Texas Motor Speedway

"I don't even know why I'm going to watch it. I know he is going to win. He has gotten so smart sitting in the [TV] booth. It's obvious that nobody else will stand a chance with all the knowledge he has gained."

–TERRY LABONTE
on Fox commentator Darrell Waltrip competing in a Craftsman Truck Series race at Martinsville

Greg Biffle was probably born too late, not that it was much of a disadvantage in 2005, when the thirty-six-year-old driver became a genuine NASCAR star.

Biffle didn't start racing go-karts when he was four. He didn't have a dad who gave up everything to make his son a star. He started banging around on short tracks when he was a teenager. When Jack Roush signed him to a contract, he was running a restaurant on the side to raise some extra cash to go racing.

His story doesn't sound familiar anymore. Many of Biffle's peers only go to restaurants where they park your car for you. They hire someone to flip the burgers at their motor coaches, and that's when they want to try some "quaint" American cuisine.

"I didn't really say I wanted to be a race driver, per se, but I loved to drive anything that had four wheels and tires and a gas pedal," Biffle says. "When I was ten years old, I'm driving up and down the road, back and forth. We had some property and my grandmother lived at the end of the road, so I was taking the car and driving back and forth, and riding my motorcycle every day. I loved to ride my motorcycle.

"I begged my dad for a go-kart about once a week. He probably got tired of hearing it, but I didn't have any place to ride it if I'd had one . . . I had that interest and I watched the racing, but I didn't really connect the two—like, 'that's what I'm going to do'—until I was in high school and started racing oval track, hobby stock, street stocks. That's when I kind of got the bug."

Biffle had a knack for it. That's the only way he could have gotten this far this fast. People look at him and can't believe he's thirty-six, but for a guy who started out with nothing—no rich dad paying the bills, no big-shot racer behind him—he's risen to the top in quite a hurry.

He's old school, and when you ask him about it, he says, "Yeah, pretty much."

It almost makes you want to ask if Biffle ever "ran 'shine down in Alabam'," but then you remember he's from Vancouver, Washington, and that the illegal-liquor trade was probably kind of sparse in the Northwest, although there probably was some bootlegging from across the Canadian border back during Prohibition.

On a Friday morning in Phoenix, Biffle wasn't pleased with his car, so he did what racers used to do. He stewed over the matter with his crew chief, Doug Richert, and the two drank coffees at the crack of dawn because neither could get any sleep for worrying about it. Of course, racers didn't used to have posh motor coaches in the infield. There are limits to old school. Biffle and Richert didn't get together at a diner. They got together in the coach.

"I was drinking my coffee and reading the paper, and we kept talking about the car for about forty-five minutes," Biffle says. "I didn't see any other drivers or any other crew chiefs doing that."

He ought to know. They were all parked nearby.

"I never said I *could* drive."

–TERRY LABONTE

asked how he felt toward those who said
he couldn't drive anymore

"I'm going to party all night, and I don't even
drink. Lots of Gatorade, I guess. I may never
win another one."

–MARK MARTIN
after winning the 2002 Coca-Cola 600

When Tony Stewart debuted in the Cup Series and enjoyed immediate success, he said it was because the Cup cars were easier for him to drive than the ones in the Busch Series. He still feels that way.

"I still think, from my aspect, it was probably easier to get used to the Cup car just because of the horsepower differences," he said. "The Busch cars' straightaway speeds are a little slower so you drive it a lot deeper into the corners than you do with the Cup cars. I still believe it was easier for me to make the transition from the sprint cars and midgets to the Cup Series versus the Busch Series.

"Now, having the Cup Series experience on my side, it does make it easier to go to the Busch Series and know what to expect once I get there now. So it's kind of a backwards leap if you think about skipping the Busch and going to Cup and then backwards."

"I had the big old piece of cake on my fork,
and it fell right off on the floor."

–JIMMIE JOHNSON

**after making a pit road error that cost
him the 2002 Coca-Cola 600**

Lhe combination of a pair of legends, Junior Johnson and Darrell Waltrip, dominated stock car racing for most of the 1980s. Out of the 132 victories credited to cars owned by Johnson, Waltrip won 43, not to mention championships in 1981, 1982, and 1985.

Johnson had himself been one of NASCAR's premier drivers prior to his retirement in 1966. Dubbed "the last American hero" by author Tom Wolfe in a 1965 *Esquire* article, Johnson began his racing career as an avocation. NASCAR founder William H. G. France tried to persuade him to run a full schedule by saying he wanted Johnson to "commit" himself.

As recounted by Johnson, his reply to France was, "I'm not committed to racing. I'm a bootlegger. I don't race on the track; I race down the highway. It's the same situation as when you're having bacon and eggs for breakfast. That bacon comes from the pig. He was committed. The egg comes from a chicken. She was involved.

"Where NASCAR was concerned, at that time, I was involved."

What led Johnson to become committed was a stint in federal prison, one that ended just a few months before he won the 1960 Daytona 500. He retired as a driver in 1966 after winning fifty races.

When Waltrip took over as driver of Johnson's number 11 Chevrolet in 1981, he brought his attorney along to negotiate a contract. Johnson and Waltrip, along with their attorneys, met in a dimly lit law office in North Wilkesboro, North Carolina. Waltrip was astonished when he discovered that his new contract was only a page in length.

"My lawyer felt like we were dealing with a couple of hillbillies," Waltrip recalls. "The contract wasn't much more than 'you drive and I'll provide the car.' My lawyer asked Junior, 'What are you going to do for Darrell once he starts winning all the races?' Junior got that serious expression on his face, paused for a few seconds, and finally said, 'I'll tell you what I'll do to him if he don't.'"

to one of his earlier drivers, Cale Yarborough, whom Waltrip disliked.

"Can't you step it up a little, Cale?" Johnson would ask via radio.

"This ain't no damn Cale Yarborough!" Waltrip would scream back.

"That always made ol' Darrell go a little faster," Johnson says.

In the 2004 Daytona 500, Bobby Labonte's Chevrolet carried sponsorship from the movie *The Passion of the Christ*.

Actor Ben Affleck was at the race and noted the potential effect.

"[That] begs the question of the other drivers," said Affleck. "Why even show up? I mean, Jesus is in Bobby's pit. You know who's side God is on. I guess Kid Rock is going to be here, too. My money's on Jesus."

Alas, Dale Earnhardt Jr. won the 500.

Jeff Burton, making his first appearance in Richard Childress's number 30 Chevrolet, overshot his pit stall on a stop shortly before the halfway point at Michigan International Speedway in 2004.

No, that's not exactly true.

What happened, apparently, was that Burton mistakenly pulled into the stall of his former team, the number 99 Ford in which Carl Edwards had succeeded him.

During a June 2004 race at Pocono Raceway in Pennsylvania, a NASCAR official displayed a flag indicating that pit road was closed to race leader Jimmie Johnson, then opened the pits as soon as Johnson had passed, allowing everyone else to pit. The mistake cost Johnson more than a dozen positions, although he miraculously came back to win the race.

Guess Johnson didn't say, "Simon says."

"At this point, I think if I saw someone on the side of the road selling horseshoes, I would stop and buy one."

–*BOBBY LABONTE*

in the midst of a tough season

"I kind of led the team astray. I couldn't even remember being here last year. I get this place and Kansas City mixed up."

–MICHAEL WALTRIP

at Chicagoland

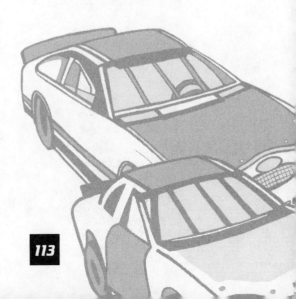

Barbecue was once the staple of the North Carolina Speedway press box. On the track's final NASCAR weekend, the fare was chicken and beef fajitas. Someone noted that one of the races went to Southern California, so California Speedway sent its food back to Rockingham.

Before the 2003 Chevy Rock & Roll 400 in Richmond, Virginia, officials put on a rock show that included appearances by Franky Perez and groups with names like Trapt, Staind and Uncle Kracker.

The music seemed sort of alien to many of those present.

Rosemary Rose, a fan wearing a "Proud to Be American" T-shirt and straw hat, said, "Putting these people onstage in front of us is unfair. This is not what I call NASCAR music."

"I've been trying to focus totally on racing and forget about the rest of the stuff. I don't want to run off and do a bunch of commercials. I don't want to do movies. I want to be right here."

—BILL ELLIOTT
after winning the 2002 Brickyard 400

"I thought maybe he needed a psychologist, first off for owning a race team and secondly for hiring me."

—BILL ELLIOTT
on Ray Evernham

"He fits my mold. I like a guy who's got some spunk and says what he believes."

—Hall of Famer

JUNIOR JOHNSON

on Tony Stewart

After Dale Earnhardt Jr.'s 2003 victory at Phoenix International Raceway, a "mystery woman" walked to the window outside the media center, banged on the window to get Junior's attention, and proceeded to lift up her T-shirt and expose herself to the race winner.

When the resulting clamor subsided, Earnhardt Jr. leaned toward the microphone and noted, "I guess the demographic of this sport is changing."

"We found about eight different ways to go the same speed."

–KURT BUSCH

after practice and qualifying at Richmond in 2002

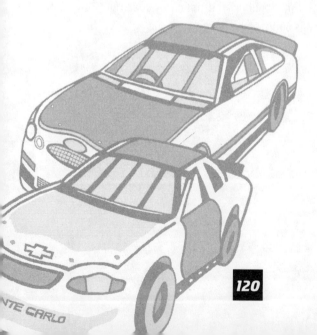

"They're going to have to come in here and bulldoze the place."

–RUSTY WALLACE

complaining about **New Hampshire**
International Speedway

NASCAR president Mike Helton, upset with Kurt Busch in 2003, revoked the young driver's "hard card," which didn't have any formal effect. It did, however, force Busch to stand in line each week at the credential stand and wait for a while after each of the season's final races so that he could turn in his "paper credentials" to Cup Series director John Darby.

In short, it was the equivalent of having Busch stay after school to write "I must not misbehave in class" several hundred times on a blackboard.

Retired air force general Tom Sadler, head of Speedway Children's Charities, told a Texas Motor Speedway crowd of 180,000 that American troops were fighting in Iraq "to defend the Second Amendment."

That particular amendment deals with the right to bear arms. The National Rifle Association is a generous contributor to Speedway Children's Charities.

Most would concede that Americans' right to bear arms was pretty clear in Iraq.

"The thing about an accident is that if you miss an accident by just an inch, it never happens. Sometimes the accident that could do you in, you don't even know about."

—JACK ROUSH

"If Richard [Childress] is satisfied and the people around me who need to be satisfied are satisfied, the rest of it really doesn't matter. That's the biggest thing that I had to understand: You can't make everyone happy."

–KEVIN HARVICK

"I really ain't doing much, just turning left every once in a while."

–DALE EARNHARDT JR.

explaining four straight victories at Talladega

"Safety is a moving target."

–JEFF BURTON

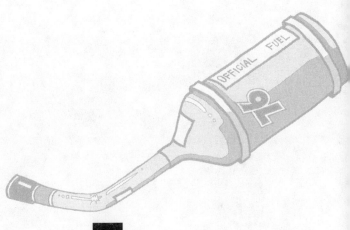

When NASCAR officials failed to throw a red flag—which would have brought the race to a temporary halt and improved the chance of a full-speed finish—at the end of the 2002 Pepsi 400 at Daytona, backstretch fans responded by hurling thousands of pieces of debris—programs, beer cans, plastic cups, and the like—onto the track while the cars slowly completed the final few laps.

Michael Waltrip mistakenly thought the fans were saluting his victory.

"Nothing has changed, but yet this year is totally different."

−BOBBY LABONTE

"I make a habit of getting myself in trouble. When I don't self-inflict the wounds, they come to me anyway."

–TONY STEWART

Eight cars in the 2002 Tropicana 400 at Chicagoland Speedway carried paint schemes devoted to the Muppets. Sponsors planned to have entertainers in Muppets costumes touring the grounds on race day, that is, until the speedway's president at the time, Joie Chitwood III, decreed that any Muppets showing up on the property would be arrested.

Apparently Chitwood felt that the speedway should be paid for allowing Muppets at the track.

Even in an age of security concerns, few people anticipated a day when someone could go to jail for "aiding and abetting a Muppet."

After a 2002 race in Bristol, Tennessee, a female fan claimed Tony Stewart pushed her out of his way. When a local sheriff got wind of it, he sent five deputies to Richmond, Virginia (the next race), to investigate the case and brought Stewart before a grand jury to face potential assault charges.

Yes, the sheriff was running for reelection at the time.

"If you pass after the caution flag, you're suscepting yourself to a penalty."

– RYAN NEWMAN

"You hit the wall head-on; it hurts . . . Some of the younger guys haven't experienced that yet."

–JOE NEMECHEK

"Yeah, it's a big track, and it's actually easier to drive around than Daytona. At Daytona, you actually have to drive a little bit. Here it feels like it's 99 percent car. Like in the old days when they sent a chimp up to fly a rocket around the world. I feel like the chimp. I'm sitting in a really good car that was prepared by really good people with a good engine."

–BORIS SAID
on Talladega Superspeedway

"I don't claim to have any answers or know the answers. We pay good money for good people to come in and build these things, but I can tell you when it don't run, and I can tell you when it does run, and that's my job and I've tried to do it."

—DALE EARNHARDT JR.

Race fans are particularly susceptible to bad weather simply because so many of them camp out at and near the tracks.

In the wee hours of April 30, 2005, a storm that was almost biblical in nature ripped through the grounds of Talladega Superspeedway. That fans endured it is perhaps the greatest testimony to their persistence and loyalty to the sport.

Tents flooded. Red-clay pools overran the bottomlands. The high ground at Gettysburg was no more crucial than in the sprawling lots of Talladega, where shirtless fans emerged to play tackle football in the muck. Then they donned T-shirts that made them vaguely presentable, loaded their coolers with frosty beverages, and made the slow march to the track, where they got rained on some more and kept their chins up, hoping to see a Busch Series race. Then they sat in the rain some more, finally watching a race that ended in virtual darkness.

Early in the morning, track president Grant Lynch had reported there were no weather-related injuries among the fans, although that may have changed had he waited for the muddy football games to commence.

A press release issued the week before the race had quoted Nextel Cup crew chief Greg Steadman as follows: "Outside of when it is actually falling and you are sitting around waiting to get on the track, rain just doesn't affect Talladega."

Tell that to the fans.

137

NASCAR fans are sensitive to the criticism that they go to the races for the crashes. They read stories in which someone who's never been to a race preaches about how race fans just go to see wrecks. And . . . the point is?

What's the big deal? Don't people go to football games to see hits? Don't they go to baseball games to see home runs? It's not rational. It's just something that attracts us.

It's more complicated than what the sport's detractors claim. The great majority of race fans are responsible, law-abiding citizens, and they certainly don't want to see people get hurt or killed. If you've ever been at a track when a serious crash occurred and you've watched the reaction in the grandstands while waiting for the driver to climb out of his mangled automobile, then you know that fans don't want to see someone hurt.

They don't want to see death. They want to see death defied. They don't want to see injury. They want to see injury defied.

Man, d'you see that? How'd that fool walk away from that wreck? Climb outta that? You can't even tell it was a car! Unbelievable, man. I gotta see me some more of this.

It's what we are. It's how we live. It's what we do. We want to see death defied. It's one of the reasons we go to the movies, buy popcorn, and sit right up front, munching away and drawing Coca-Cola through a straw, while spaceships and airplanes and robots and extraterrestrials blow things and one another up.

The movies aren't real, you say? Well, just what is the difference, in terms of the spectacle and what's being processed by all those synapses and neurons, between live and Memorex?

Racing is exciting. Spectacular passes are exciting. Wrecks are exciting.

Why do we go to amusement parks, jump out of airplanes and pull the cord, drive too fast, and go on vacation? It's to get relief from the monotony of human existence. It's to escape the mundane existence. A man can't pay bills and read e-mail and leave messages that won't get returned forever. He's got to get away.

He's got to go to Talladega, sip some cool ones, and get off his duff and yell, "Hoody-hoo!" every time Junior zips by.

If he didn't have the occasional Talladega, the stray Bristol, and the two weeks of Charlotte, no telling into what mischief he might tumble.

So let him watch his race and stop psychoanalyzing everything.